Blackberries

Story by Beverley Randell
Illustrated by Isabel Lowe

Father Bear
and Mother bear
and Baby Bear
went to look for blackberries.

4

Father Bear's blackberries went into this basket.

Mother Bear's blackberries went into this basket.

Baby Bear's blackberries went into this basket.

"Blackberries, blackberries,
I like blackberries,"
said Baby Bear.

"Where is Baby Bear?"
said Mother Bear.
"Father Bear,
is Baby Bear with you?"

"No," said Father Bear.
"Where is he?"

"Baby Bear, where are you?" shouted Father Bear.

"Baby Bear, where are you?" shouted Mother Bear.

"Here I am,"
said Baby Bear.
"I'm here."

Father Bear
looked in Baby Bear's basket.
"Where are your blackberries?"
he said.

"In here," said Baby Bear.

"Inside **me**."